Breathwork

Breathwork

HOW TO

USE

YOUR

BREATH

TO

CHANGE

YOUR

LIFE

Andrew Smart

ILLUSTRATIONS BY
Eric Nyquist

CHRONICLE BOOKS
SAN FRANCISCO

Text copyright © 2020 by Andrew Smart.
Illustration copyright © 2020 by Eric Nyquist.

Library of Congress
Cataloging-in-Publication Data available.

ISBN 978-1-4521-8122-6

Manufactured in China.

Design by Lizzie Vaughan.
Typeset by Katy Brown.
Typset in Noe and TT Norms.

10 9 8 7 6 5 4 3

Chronicle Books LLC
680 Second Street
San Francisco, CA 94107
www.chroniclebooks.com

Dedication

To a fourth dimension.
May you be rocketed there.

PART I

Inhale

PART II

Exhale

A Life on Breath

A book about breath is a book about life.

I definitely had a life before I discovered breathwork. And I have one after. It's the manner in which I live it that has changed. In some ways, the changes are subtle; in others, profound.

At this point, I'm very certain of one thing: However I'm breathing is however I'm living. If I find myself holding my breath, I'm likely holding back, controlling, siphoning off energy from my creativity and my most important relationships. If my breath is shallow, I'm not reaching the most powerful depths in spirituality, in work, and in love.

When I first discovered breathwork, I was recently sober. Raw would be an understatement. I came into it with zero expectations. In fact, at my first session, I thought we were all coming together to sit down for a quiet, guided meditation.

Instead, it was something altogether different. It was activating, intense, difficult. From an energetic standpoint, I felt my sternum breaking open, revealing my heart for the first time. I felt ecstasy and agony. And while, in life, I had known unconditional love, during this breathwork session, I felt it for the first time. As the great Dutch athlete and breathwork pioneer Wim Hof says, "Feeling is understanding." And in this altered state—cultivated 100 percent without drugs—I escaped the thinking mind for a time and experienced spirituality firsthand. I instantly released long-held resentments. I left my body and watched myself from a bird's-eye view, lying on a concrete floor, breathing deeply, and laughed at the beauty and comedy that is life on Earth. My mind, body, and spirit were blown.

It took months for me to try it again. But after a period of fear and resistance (and with the encouragement of a few great guides—Ann Faison, Lauren Spencer King, and David Elliott), I accepted that if I was going to find whatever I was looking for in life, I would find it riding the breath.

So I studied. And I practiced. And then I began teaching others.

Every time I hold space (guide another person or a group through a session of breath), my eyes are opened to something I hadn't seen before. The breath keeps changing, and I keep changing along with it. Every time I breathe, I learn something new. What's captured here is what I know of the power of breath so far.

The following pages are organized into two sections: Inhale and Exhale. Part One: Inhale includes seven chapters, counting up from chapter 1, that reflect some of the feelings, sensations, experiences, troubles, and archetypes that might enter your life as you embark on a path of breath. Part Two: Exhale includes seven chapters, counting down from chapter 7, on different practices of breath—from most heady to most physical.

These practices are accessible to all readers: If you're alive, you can breathe. You have to. I encourage you to try all of the schools of breathwork presented here. And, if you find yourself drawn to a particular practice, go for it. You can experiment alone or find a trusted group. In my own practice, I have pulled elements from all seven of the schools of breath outlined in Part Two into my daily breathwork practice.

The best way for you to use this book is to let your intuition guide you. Whatever you have to learn, to feel, to understand is already inside you. You don't need a class or permission from a guru to enter. You don't need psychedelic drugs. And you don't need this book. But I really hope you enjoy it anyway.

Inhale

1

You Can Take a Breath

A beloved yoga teacher, Eddie Ellner,
often opens his class with the words,
"You can take a breath."

This is an invitation.

And a reminder.

Did you forget you can breathe right now?
Did you lose sight of how amazing that is?

"You can take a breath" is a cue to add
consciousness to something you're already
doing, to take something automatic and
make it intentional.

You'll take millions of breaths in a lifetime.
But what about *this one*?

Will it be nothing more than the breath
between the last one and the next one?
Or will you empower it to be something more?

If you're feeling anxious, you can take a breath. If you're feeling physically tight or run-down, you can take a breath. If you're feeling disconnected from others, from the experience of your own life, or from your own understanding of God, you can take a breath. In every moment, good or bad, you can always take a breath.

TRY IT NOW.

Inhale deeply.

Exhale. Repeat.

Try it again.

Breathe all the way in. Let it go. Again. That's how we feed our systems. That's how we open our hearts, let go of stress and anxiety, and live full, happy lives. We breathe.

Breath is the antidote to our digital "lifestyle." Breath connects us to our MAGIC, to our ability to heal ourselves and others, to our untapped creativity. It adds gravity to the words of Carl Sagan, who said, "We are made of star-stuff." The breath can take us back to the beginning of time. It can whisper big truths in our ears. It can show us the impossible. It can reconnect us with ancient cycles driven by the force of the sun and the pull of the moon. It can help us heal. It can get us closer to whatever force we believe rules the universe. It can show us unconditional love. And it can remind us how to be human.

You can take a breath.

Take the next one like

your life depends on it.

Because it does.

"There is one way of breathing that is shameful and constricted. Then, there's another way: a breath of love that takes you all the way to infinity."

—Rumi

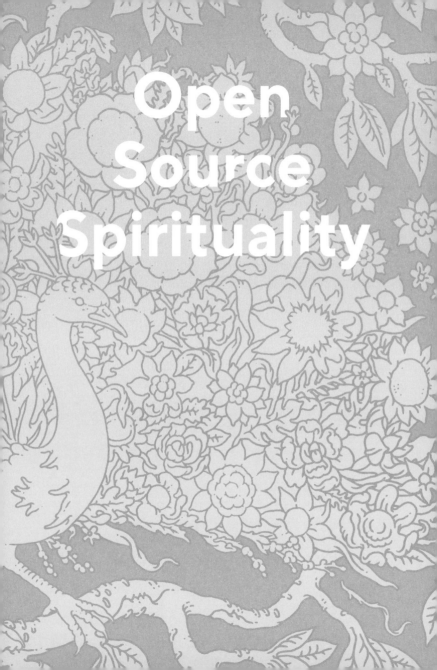

Open
Source
Spirituality

What exactly is breathwork?

Breathwork is open source spirituality. No gurus needed. No thousand-dollar mantras required. No equipment. No structure. No church. Can you breathe? Can you count to four? You're in! Welcome to the club.

You don't breathe because you want to. You breathe because you have to. Breath isn't a choice. It's a biological imperative. It's the first thing you do when you arrive here on Earth. And it's the last thing you do before leaving. When you take that last one, that's it. To the best of our knowledge, that's the end of "you."

What exactly is "you"? If you exist when breathing and you don't when not, what's the difference, if not a combination of oxygen, nitrogen, and other gases filtered through the lungs and distributed throughout the body?

When the breath stops, life stops. No breath equals no life. And that makes breath a very, very big deal.

Try more breath.

Breathing becomes *breathwork* when you add attention and energy to it. Breathwork is the simple act of becoming aware of the breath. Breathing in a specific pattern is breathwork. Breathing powerfully and intensely for a preset period of time, that's also breathwork. If you have any kind of regular meditation routine or yoga practice, you're already doing a form of breathwork. If you slow down your breath during cardiovascular training, that's breathwork, too.

Some breathwork practices date back to ancient times, like *pranayama*, a yogic breath practice developed in India, or heat-creating *tummo*, a high-intensity practice from high-altitude Tibet. And then there are breath practices that are quite "new" by comparison, like Holotropic Breathwork, developed more recently by the Czech psychiatrist and explorer of psychedelia Stanislav Grof.

2

Open Source Spirituality

We'll get into some of these—and more—breathwork schools and modalities in the pages ahead. But be assured, breathwork isn't some new cure-all technology fad dreamed up at Burning Man and dropped down upon us by our Silicon Valley overlords.

It's not a religion. And it's not in conflict with your religion. The poet Rumi was a Muslim. Rumi did breathwork.

Thomas Merton, who said, "What I do is live, how I pray is breathe, what I wear is pants," was a Trappist monk. Thomas Merton did breathwork.

In fact, almost all religions from all corners of the world include an exaltation of breath. The word "spirituality" itself derives from the Latin word *spirare*, meaning, drumroll, to breathe.

Whether you're Buddhist, Sufi, Christian, Satanist, agnostic—however you identify on the organized religion spectrum—if you want to make a deeper spiritual connection, breathe more deeply.

If you believe in the power of prayer, try a few rounds of breath before you pray. See if your prayers become clearer, broader, more inclusive, more aligned to the common good. For many, breathwork will guide you to a greater sense of spiritual clarity. And, regardless of your religion or belief system, this newfound absence

2

Inhale

of spiritual confusion can feel a lot like channeling God. Or something akin to it.

If you want to get busy living, get busy breathing. You don't have to join anything. You don't have to renounce anything. You don't have to pay one cent to anyone. You just have to be willing to pull more air into your lungs. Breath is freely available. Breath is an expeditor. It's a catalyst. It's the moving walkway at the airport of spiritual seeking. If you give it some elbow grease, it's an effin' flux capacitor.

EVEN FIVE MINUTES can change the way you see the world and experience this unique moment in the life of you. Twenty-five minutes might find you communing with your spirit animal in an alternate, angelic reality.

But you've got to put in the work to find out.

Open Source Spirituality

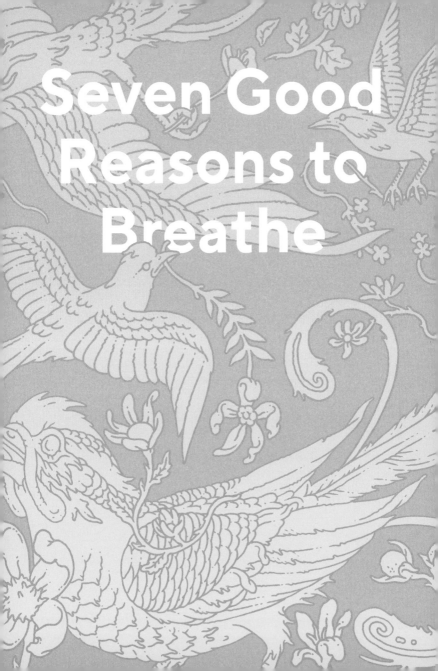

Seven Good Reasons to Breathe

Without a doubt, there are more than just seven reasons to drop everything you're doing and start breathing.

Your Twitter feed is likely full of them. But if tasks you typically find easy and enjoyable—at work, at home, or in romantic relationships—are suddenly a total drag, your energy could likely benefit from a little system reboot via breath. Here are just a few of the myriad good reasons to breathe right now.

1. CHANGE THE CHANNEL

We all get stuck.

We're focused on one

particular thing when we

would rather be focused

on literally anything else.

We're in work mode when we want to be in vacation mode. We're dwelling on the past. We're tripping on the future. We find ourselves on the outside, looking in. The not-in-the-moment affliction finds us in the boardroom. And—even worse—it finds us in the bedroom.

New-age speak tells us to "be present."

Great advice.

Not an easy task, though, in a world where Wi-Fi follows us everywhere and in a culture in which we wear our "always on" mentalities like some kind of dystopian badge of honor. In the rare moments when we actually do want to turn off, we can't. We don't remember how.

A lifetime of meditation can help us get there. But sometimes we don't have a lifetime. We need to change the channel right now. If only there were a magic switch we could just flip to be right here, right in the moment, to soak up every passing second like it's the only second.

It's not magic. And it's not a switch, per se. But breath can expedite a trip back to the present, sending more oxygenated blood to the brain and shaking loose any energy stagnating in the body.

Every time you find yourself in a thought pattern that isn't serving you, you can lie down or sit down and breathe. This can be subtle (e.g., breathing for five minutes to get your mind off of a deadline or a parking ticket, or transitioning from Workday You to Dinner with the Fam You).

Or it can be more ambitious in nature (e.g., breathing for twenty minutes to really reset, effect a mind-set shift, and breathe life into an alternate outlook on things).

So often, we have a goal or a task we need to accomplish, but our attention is elsewhere. Whether you're caught in the perpetual social media scroll or a loop of negative thinking, breathwork can become your "Stop, drop, and roll" for getting out of whatever you're lost in and getting back into the moment. It works. And it so often reminds us that our thoughts are just thoughts, reshaping what we think of as problems into opportunities for growth, and maybe even a little bit of fun.

2. OPEN YOUR HEART
The heart is a complicated organ.

It opens. It closes.

It has its own electrical system. The heart is a transmitter. Its signal is carried in the blood. Oxygenated blood has a higher pH and more energy. And the body, mind, and spirit it feeds all love that.

No doubt, an open heart feels good. It gives us an opportunity to be more compassionate with others and ourselves. It gives us an opportunity to love and be loved. But it comes with a lot of vulnerability. And life is hard. For a lot of us, it makes sense to close off the heart. We've been burned by bad relationships, family and career disappointments. Work can be a total drag. A lot of times, we just don't feel safe out there. So, it seems easier to use our big, beautiful brains to power ourselves through life. We shield our heart in so many ways, consciously and subconsciously, closing it off to the world with hunched-over posture, and limiting the love we can feel. In an effort to keep the darkness out, we lock out the light.

Does your heart need to be open all the time? Probably not. But, since the anatomical organ is a pump with a binary setting (i.e., in and out), perhaps it's at least fair to shoot for a heart that's open as often as it's closed.

To open the heart, you just need to breathe, vigorously pulling energy up the thoracic spine, over the back of the pericardial region, with focused, animated attention. A crowded subway car is probably not the right place for this. Instead, you want to create a space that is safe for you to be open and vulnerable, to feel your feelings! Or find somewhere where that kind of space is held for you (see Groups and Gurus, page 54).

When you open the heart, you'll be amazed by what gets out—grief, resentment, anger, fear, shame—and especially by what gets in (compassion, self-love, and healing).

3. GET INTO YOUR BODY

"I need to get into my body"

is a common refrain in the

breathwork universe.

But what does that even mean? Aren't we always in our bodies? Where else could we possibly be?

It seems "getting into the body" loosely translates to getting out of the head and breaking out of conditioned habits of physical tightness. An always-on-autopilot life setting may leave us with a sense of being locked out of experiencing our own lives. Sure, there's always work to be done, deadlines to meet, emails to send. But when we are locked in our minds, we are reactive rather than conscious, rather than intuitive. Getting into the body can help us return to a primal sense of feeling. Getting into the body can help us integrate our feelings harmoniously into a broader story, into conscious living and conscious action.

This concept—that the body, mind, and spirit can achieve harmony—is understood in the Tantric tradition via the chakras, a holistic system of seven individual energy centers located throughout the body, each with its own set of physical, emotional, and spiritual functions. Similarly, Traditional Chinese medicine

3

Seven Good Reasons to Breathe

focuses on the body's meridians, through which *chi* flows in a healthy system or doesn't in a body that is depressed, fatigued, or diseased.

When something gets stuck in the body—due to trauma or misalignment or lack of use—the flow of energy throughout the entire body can be stifled. A lack of energy in one area might deplete the whole system. Or too much energy in one area might result in obsessive thinking or compulsive behaviors.

In the same way a chiropractic adjustment, an acupuncture session, or craniosacral therapy can return you to a whole body state of flow, so can the breath. A trained set of eyes—paired with a developed intuition—can see where energy isn't flowing. Very often, these blocks manifest in the throat, the heart, and the lower abdomen, where sexual and creative fires want to burn hottest.

After breathing, areas of the body you didn't even realize were tight might suddenly crack and pop. Sweet release. After breathing, the words you have been searching for might find their way to the tip of your tongue. You may find yourself suddenly heart-oriented, more open to loving and being loved. And you may tap into a reserve of sexual energy, feeling an increased libido or willingness and desire to create—life or art—as the mojo starts to reclaim its natural flow.

Oxygenating the system feels good, enlivening. It can wake up areas of the body you didn't realize were fast asleep. Similar to the sensation of runner's high (healthy) or taking MDMA (not healthy), breath can send a rush of endorphins through the whole body. For those prone to overthinking, a daily breathwork practice can be both a reprieve from the ever-chattering mind and a powerful invitation to include the whole human system—from tip to tail—in the way you process and deal with all the stimuli and situations life throws your way.

The body has its own knowledge. Breathe into it. And listen.

4. KICK-START YOUR IMMUNE SYSTEM
The "science" of breathwork

is an ever-developing area of study.

Thanks to the clinical work of scientists and the breath-work pioneer Wim Hof (see Exhale, chapter 3), the world is learning more and more about the healing powers of breath. That Hof (and others) can control their autono-mous immune systems has caused a stir and rewritten the rules in the often staid medical community.

What we know for sure is this: In the natural world and in the body, more acidic environments breed disease. Hyperoxygenation—in the form of vigorous breathwork— significantly increases the pH of your blood, making it less acidic and more alkaline.

Since the blood touches all of the organs—and the immune system—its being less acidic has got to be a good thing. People spend big bucks on filters to increase the pH of their drinking water to foster a more alkaline physiological environment. Breath is another way there.

Furthermore, mitochondria—organelles that create the energy (adenosine triphosphate, or ATP) that feeds your cells—eat oxygen. So, well-fed mitochondria carry more energy to your cells, staving off illness and making you more vigorous, virile, and literally red-blooded. If your immune system is depleted, rest is good, and so is more energy. As Hof contends, if we breathe only enough to *maintain* the body, there's no energy left to *heal* the body.

Ask yourself if you feel stronger and healthier after breathing. If the answer is "yes," then you probably are. And if you feel happier and less depressed after breathwork, remember that happy people are more resistant to viruses like the common cold than people who aren't. If you start a regular breathwork practice, will you never get sick again? Unlikely. Is there a good chance you'll get sick less and beat back illnesses faster? Absolutely.

5. PROCESS YOUR GRIEF
As human animals, we shield ourselves from pain instinctively.

If we have our wits about us, our intuition guides us away from situations where we might get hurt. We don't foolishly approach a growling dog. We don't have to touch a hot stove burner more than once to know not to try that again. We're built to evolutionary specification to shy away from pain in the present. Thus, it's only natural that we so often are willing to do anything and everything we can to avoid hurts from the past.

The pain of loss is part of the human condition. We lose family. We lose friends. We lose dreams. We lose innocence. We lose security. We lose time. Every life has its losses. If we don't process the feelings that come up around loss, their energy can build up inside us. Our demeanor, our posture, our health—even our whole being—can be determined by what we've lost and from avoiding the feelings that come with it. A lot of us— especially men—have been told over and over again to bury our sadness: "chin up," "stiff upper lip." The sadness that underlies a lot of our other emotions—like anger—can result in our most destructive behaviors. Think: addiction, codependence, and overeating.

Breathwork gives us a platform and an opportunity to feel sadness. To let it touch us. And to let it go. Real bravery isn't a superhuman capacity to hold it together. It's a willingness to actually feel. Breathwork opens energetic doors to a safe place where you can grieve a lost loved one, a failed relationship, even a period of your life (e.g., middle school, ugh) that you can never return to. If you hold on too tightly to hurt, the heart has no energetic appendages left to embrace anything else—be it a new love or a passion project.

At a breathwork session, you might be encouraged to "let go of your face." This is a physical cue to relax your jaw, let your cheeks sag, and allow your forehead to melt. But it's also a directive to literally release the face you believe you need to present to the world. With this permission to not have to be anything to anyone—and the heart-opening power of breath—you can be with your loss. You can remove its claws and fangs and find the beauty in it. If you're open and willing, you'll get to bawl your eyes out, experiencing firsthand the spiritual, physical, and emotional refreshment of flushing the system with a good cry.

In the healing community, you'll come across a lot of empaths (if you're really drawn to breathwork, you probably are one).

Empaths are highly sensitive, highly intuitive people. They are stickier than others. Their bodies attempt to process the sadness, anger, and shame of others. And they pick up energies along the way that aren't theirs. These external energies—even entities—made internal can drain us of our life force.

If you've ever felt creeped out by something you couldn't quite put your finger on, walked into a room and immediately felt the need to get out, or returned home from lunch with a friend feeling totally drained and exhausted, you've probably picked up some psychospiritual trash. The energy of a bad relationship or a less-than-ideal interpersonal exchange can linger. An encounter with an angry person can have you feeling angry. An encounter out in the world with an anxious person finds you running their anxiety when you get back home. An encounter with an "energetic vampire" or malignant narcissist can leave you

3

| Seven Good Reasons to Breathe

feeling more depleted and more vulnerable than you really are.

With practice, you can learn to see and feel what's yours and what isn't. And you can shield yourself from unwanted energies with a silent (or not-so-silent), resounding "no." It's not the empath's responsibility to take on other people's shit. As an empath, it's not your responsibility to process your mother's disappointments or the sexual trauma of a stranger on the subway.

Think of breathwork as a salt bath for the spirit, an opportunity to reclaim the sanctity and autonomy of your personal space. Breathwork can reset the invisible barriers between "us" and "out there," a subject brilliantly outlined by Cyndi Dale in her book *Energetic Boundaries.*

Breathwork enables the release of what isn't ours, so we can let go of projected belief systems that don't serve us. There are forces at work that don't want us living our best life. While some situations are simply a "mind fuck," the more complicated ones are a "soul fuck." A trusted friend and guide once observed, "Spiritual warfare is real." In breathwork, we can assume the role of spiritual warrior, sharpening the weapons in our arsenal so we can protect the sanctity of our spirits—and of others'—and lead the way, lighting the path forward with compassion and love.

7. TRIP OUT

There's a reason people in the psychedelic and plant medicine communities seem to crawl out of their drum circles and show up at breathwork.

"I got so high" is a common reaction from first-timers to breathwork, as they crack open their heart, temporarily silence the thinking mind, and expose and awaken sleeping receptors for endorphins, adrenaline, and serotonin in the body. The result can be a kind of physical euphoria, a vibrating, tingling experience of *more*.

At a three-hour Holotropic Breathwork experience, for example, one might have sensations that sure do feel like the serotonin rush of "rolling" on MDMA, or the colorful delight of a "trip" on psilocybin mushrooms or DMT, a naturally occurring psychedelic chemical found in the human body. Or even better, maybe a little of all of the above. All of this is available to some people after just a few minutes of active breath. These drug-like sensations are by no means limited to only those who have tried the aforementioned substances. If drugs have never been your thing—good for you—

3

Seven Good Reasons to Breathe

these experiences might be more in line with the realms of dreams or sex or intense physical exertion (i.e., runner's high). The point is, your body is already equipped to achieve an altered state, naturally. The more open you are, the more likely it is that you'll be able to break out of the constraints the ego puts in place to protect you.

The "trippy" aspect of breathwork can also manifest as dreamlike narratives or vivid visitations from ancestors, spirit guides, and animal guides. In this case, it seems the subconscious becomes—for a time—conscious. You might totally lose your sense of time and space.

In this altered state, you can learn a lot about yourself. In the same way it's good to keep a pencil and a pad on your nightstand to write down your dreams, it's good to make a note of what bubbles up from the subconscious on the breath.

You might have an out-of-body experience in which you experience yourself and the space you are in at an extraordinary distance. If floating above your body while watching lightning bolts firing from your acupuncture points sounds appealing, then breathwork might be for you.

It's worth cautioning here that expecting a trip is an excellent way not to get one. It's a possibility. Not a guarantee. So, it's good to be open to whatever comes up. The secret to happiness is, of course, low expectations. But none is even better. And it's worth cautioning here that in the world of breathwork—just as in life—it's possible to get caught up in constantly chasing experiences that are "more intense," while missing the beauty and profound wisdom in the subtle.

If the idea of losing control brings up uneasiness for you, that's worth exploring.

Breathwork may be too intense for some with certain psychological conditions. For others—especially those in addiction recovery—it is their most trusted respite from a difficult psychological reality. We'll talk more about this subject in chapter 6 (see page 63). But one thing is for sure: Sound and music can be great conductors of pseudopsychedelic experiences. At breathwork circles, you may hear everything from Native American pan flute to Tibetan chanting to acid house to ambient stylings by the likes of Brian Eno and Aphex Twin. Experiment and set the mood with sounds that take you out of yourself.

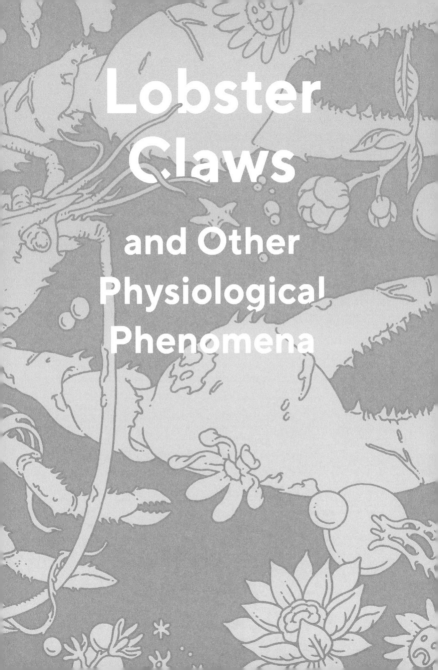

Lobster
Claws

and Other
Physiological
Phenomena

While every breather will have an entirely different experience each time they breathe,

Here are a few common physical sensations that may come up in the breath.

It's common to experience a range of physical sensations, some exceedingly pleasurable, others not so much. Even in a relatively short session of breathing, you might experience feelings that fall on both ends of the spectrum. Often, when getting started, your natural resistance to the practice might serve up some discomfort— both physical and emotional. But if you keep breathing and break through that initial stage of struggle, you might find unfettered joy on the other side.

1. TINGLING

Often in the first few minutes of vigorous breathing, you might feel a tingling sensation as the body begins to wake up.

For some, this can be very pleasurable. For others, it might feel like their hands and feet—in some cases their whole body—has gone all pins and needles. In most cases, any prickly sensations will disappear at some point during your breathing session. In rare cases, your hands may still be tingling even hours after breathing. If this happens with you, it's recommended you drink some water, eat some grounding food (think: root vegetables), and do activities that are grounding—walking barefoot, meditation, stretching, literally making conscious contact with the earth beneath you, etc.

2. TETANY

In some seemingly extreme scenarios, you'll experience a phenomenon known as *tetany*.

Tetany occurs as a result of hyperoxygenation. It most often manifests as extreme tightness in the hands, the mouth, or both. While first-timers seem most prone to tetany, you may encounter it at any time as you go deeper into your practice.

In the hands, tetany can contort your fingers into what may be described as "lobster claws," rendering them useless as the fingers squeeze together in a five-digit point. While this level of vulnerability can be discon-certing and sometimes painful, it's recommended that you continue to breathe while relaxing the muscles between your shoulder blades. Those who experience tetany in the hands often also have a heavy heart—they've lost a loved one, or a relationship has recently fallen apart. This type of tetany is an invitation to fully mourn someone or something. From a spiritual and energetic perspective, it seems to be linked to holding on to something with the heart, such as a love lost. You may find that if you continue to breathe, open the heart, and allow the subconscious to work through the sensation, the hands will release.

4

—

Inhale

Others will experience tetany around the mouth. The lips will purse and pucker into an uncomfortable kiss. While it can be difficult—sometimes nearly impossible—to continue to breathe through the mouth, you can always shift to breathing through the nose.

Often those who experience tetany around the mouth are carrying something unsaid, something to get off their chest, words and feelings unexpressed. If you find your lips closing shut during a session of breathwork, it can be helpful to ask yourself what you really need to say: Perhaps it's an apology, perhaps it's letting someone know how much they hurt you, or perhaps it's offering forgiveness to someone who let you down. Tetany around the lips can be an energetic invitation to speak your truth. This can come in the form of a phone call, writing, singing, etc. Regardless, it's very possible that a daily magnesium supplement can reduce the discomfort and severity of this occurrence during breathwork.

3. TEMPERATURE FLUCTUATION

During a breathwork session, you may experience major fluctuations in temperature sensation.

It's always good to have a blanket nearby if you get cold and to wear layers you can shed if you break a sweat as energy starts moving through your body.

4. EUPHORIA

Many people come back to the breath because of the electrifying, illuminating "body high" they experience.

This sensation of empowering oneness can have us feeling lit up, even ecstatic. Should you find yourself in a state of boundless euphoria, it's recommended that you let yourself enjoy it and recognize that all things pass—even the good things.

4

Inhale

5. PAIN

Sometimes you might feel discomfort somewhere in the body during breathwork.

It might manifest in the arms or legs, in the neck, or in the chest. Often these are areas where we hold a lot of tension, tension that is being exposed by the breath. While the rest of your body is opening up, these muscles seem to be holding on for dear life.

Try to relax the area. If you can't do that, relax the muscles around it. Commit to breathing with more intensity and mentally send the force of the breath where the tension is. You can also try exhaling on the mantra "letting go." It can also help to do some bodywork on yourself. You don't have to be a certified massage therapist. Use your intuition and apply firm pressure to the offending area while breathing deeply into your fingertips. You may induce a deep physical release— and often an accompanying emotional release.

4

Lobster Claws

51

6. LAUGHTER AND TEARS

You may break out in laughter.

You may break down in tears.

The emotional release set off by breath is the result of what happens when you stop being mind-oriented (controlling) and start being heart-centered (receptive). We all know that laughter is good for us and that nothing cleanses like a good cry. If you're in a group setting and emotion comes up, the recommendation is to let go of any need to "keep it together," and let loose. You'll feel better afterward.

7. RELAXATION

For some, a breathwork session will be the only time during a busy week when you have time to truly rest.

Most of the time, breathwork is energizing. If you feel depleted going in, you may feel activated going out. On some occasions, though, the body will get heavy and you'll drop into a kind of trancelike near sleep, known as *yoga nidra*. This can be an incredibly healing, restoring place to be. In a group setting, you may be encouraged to breathe your way out of slumber, back into a peak experience of some kind. In my philosophy, if you need to rest, rest.

4

Lobster Claws

Groups
and Gurus

One of the best ways to get into breathwork is to find a group (or "circle") or a class that meets near where you live.

Often you can find these groups at yoga studios. There are also groups that meet online, via the magic of the Internet. Groups can be highly effective at getting you into the room, onto the mat, and into the breath. They provide a set time where you can dedicate yourself to breath. They often feature guidance from an experienced teacher or facilitator. Like a writer's group or a runner's group, a breathwork group can keep us honest, dedicated, and present. And breathing with others can help us get out of our own heads and deeper into the experience of breath.

that while group energy can

be totally amazing, it can also

be challenging.

No two groups that meet to breathe are ever exactly the same. Every group has its own distinct energy. The same group's energy will be totally different on a Friday night than it is on a Sunday morning. This group energy—or personality—can be as much as who shows up in the room as what the moon is doing in the sky. Groups breathing under a full moon can get especially intense.

In a group setting, you may find the breathing of others distracting. Those around you may moan or growl or weep. Most often, though, the collective energy of the group is focusing and encouraging, showing us the beautiful, complicated humanity we all have in common instead of the little things that set us apart. If hearing another person weeping is triggering for you,

5

Groups and Gurus

perhaps it's exactly where you need to be triggered. If your response is, "I should help that person," it's probably good to look at areas of your life where you put the needs of others ahead of your own. And, whether you find yourself illuminated by others in the room or completely put off by them, keep in mind that everyone has the capacity to be a mirror, that these characters might have been put in front of you for a reason.

Usually, the energy in the room is distinctly different after breathing than it was before. Sometimes, it seems caffeinated, exuberant, as people exit the building excited and chatty. Other times, the energy is watery; it takes people a long time to peel themselves off the floor, and they exit in silence.

Often there will be an opportunity to share your experience and feelings before or after breathing. This can be a chance to express yourself honestly and get some group therapy of sorts. But it can also provide a platform for certain individuals to impose their will (consciously or subconsciously) on the group or attempt to take control of the group narrative (i.e., make it all about them). Anytime you find yourself in a group setting— whether breathing or not—good boundaries are important. It's always beneficial to be grounded in self and clear about where you end and the group begins. If you are an empath, it's especially important not to make yourself available to process the feelings of others in the group.

You don't need a teacher to breathe.

It's all already in you. But a guided environment can offer both comfort and motivation, and a set time for breathing you can clear in your busy schedule. Also, paying twenty bucks—or way more for a one-on-one session—for the pleasure can give the breath a distinct value, enough to encourage you to really do the work and get the highest return on your investment.

A good facilitator should seem grounded, openhearted, and clear-headed. If that's not the case and, say, the teacher's energy seems frenetic, perhaps find another one.

A trained facilitator can help guide you through your blocks. They might spot areas of your body where energy isn't moving and encourage you to direct your attention there, or place a hand on your body, or offer a slight adjustment. They also might offer verbal encouragement if you've lost the rhythm of your breath or fallen into a kind of slumber. Some teachers might work Reiki, bodywork (such as targeted massage), crystals, or gongs into the experience. They'll also be a

5

Groups and Gurus

DJ, playing music intended to get you into a rhythm or push you toward an altered state.

There are teachers out there who have a lot of experience. They seem extra woke, extra attuned. They seem to be channeling energy from ethereal realms. They've developed their intuition in a manner that lets them "just know" what's going on in your body, psyche, and energetic field. This can be alluring and beguiling, no doubt.

But, while some guru types may seem like holy men or holy women (and some actually might be), it's often just that they've already put in the hard work. At one point, they were just like you. The best teachers believe only you can be your greatest teacher, only you can be your greatest healer. If you find someone like that with whom you connect, please take advantage of it, work with them, ask them questions, pick their brain, and follow their example.

But be careful not to project too much power on them.

A GREAT TEACHER CAN SHOW YOU HOW TO HEAL YOURSELF.

They can listen.

They can watch.

But they can't do the work for you.

It can be easy to project onto leaders and authority figures (even authority figures in a yoga studio). Giving the leader too much credit for what you're doing for yourself devalues the work that you're doing. In a group environment designed for receptivity and self-reflection, it's possible to observe your own issues with authority. This can especially shed light on the way you behave in relationships with parents, mentors, and the people for whom you work.

Remember: The best teachers out there can absolutely, 100 percent, guide you toward going deeper into breath and unlocking your human and spiritual potential.

BUT THEY CAN'T BREATHE FOR YOU.

5

Groups and Gurus

Drugs

For some, breathwork can be a healthy alternative to a couple cocktails on a Friday night.

For a lot of people, breathwork takes the edge off a lot better than a six-pack or a pill ever did. And without the hangover, dehydration, and bubble-up of anxiety that can follow a big night out.

The more you breathe, the less you may find yourself tripped up by the things that led you to a drink or a drug in the first place—social anxiety, work stress, existential boredom, a lack of a spiritual connection, etc.

psychedelic drugs and experiences

are resurgent and ascendant

like never before.

What was once considered solely the rainbow-hued territory of Deadheads is now mainstream. Controlled substances like MDMA and ketamine are being used to treat depression, chronic pain, and PTSD to great (and clinically verified) effect. You may know someone who has experimented with microdosing LSD (i.e., taking a very small amount of it) on a daily basis. You may even be microdosing right now.

Ayahuasca ceremonies—based on a traditional spiritual ceremony practiced by communities in the Amazon— are now happening in Brooklyn townhouses and what seems like everywhere else. Quite a few people who have found their way to a breathwork practice started with ayahuasca, a brew made from the *Banisteriopsis*

6

Drugs

caapi shrub. When ingested, the "dream drug," DMT, is released. This chemically induced experience of the hyperspace has led them to go deeper, naturally, via the breath. And, having tried to go deeper both with plant medicine and without, they believe breath is the best way to reach an altered state, legally, and without some of the side effects (or the puke bucket!).

Holotropic Breathwork—developed by pioneering psychedelic psychiatrist Stanislav ("Stan") Grof—was created because of the federal ban on LSD that went into effect in 1968. According to Michael Stone, the founder of Holotropic Breathwork LA, the "non-ordinary states of consciousness" that Grof's patients reached were incredibly healing. Since these experiences were accessible to his patients using a chemical, Grof believed one could access the same experience without LSD. The receptors in the brain can be activated in more than just one way.

With its ability to deliver kaleidoscopic mindscapes, physical euphoria, and journeys to the depths of the subconscious, breathwork is definitely for people who love doing drugs.

But it's also for people who love doing drugs a little too much. Or a lot too much—so much that if they do drugs again, they'll likely end up institutionalized or worse.

For people whose lives have been ravaged by addiction, then touched by the power of sobriety, breathwork can be incredibly healing. Also, it's pretty fucking fun. Breathwork is a great way for sober people who have sworn off drugs and alcohol to meet their higher selves without the use of mind-altering substances. I've even heard sober people describe a breathwork session as a "freelapse."

But breathwork is more than just a druglike experience available to sober people. It actually serves to empower those in recovery to change their lives. Breathwork has become an essential part of "program" for many people in twelve-step groups that include a spiritual experience, conscious contact with a higher power, and meditation as some of their guiding principles, all of which a breath-work practice can offer. As such, it has found its way into many rehabilitation centers.

As Michael Pollan writes in *How to Change Your Mind,* "The mystical experience may just be what it feels like when you deactivate the brain's default mode network. This can be achieved . . . perhaps also by means of certain breathing exercises." Breathwork can get you closer to a God of our own understanding. It can help you get out of your own way. Or, as they say in twelve-step programs: "Let go and let God." Breathwork offers ego-dissolving powers. In areas of your life where force

6

Drugs

of will may have failed you in the past, force of breath might provide the results you are looking for.

IF YOU'RE ABOUT TO EMBARK ON A LIFE OF BREATH, CURB YOUR EXPECTATIONS.

If you heard your "friend of a friend" got super high, drug free, on breath—well, that may not happen for you.

Your experience might be one of overwhelming release of shame or an outpouring of pure gratitude and nothing else. The thing about breathwork is, it's always different. So tread lightly. We can chase the proverbial dragon with breath the same way we chased highs—and often lows—with drugs and alcohol. If you breathe for the first time and find purple beams of light emanating from your forehead while you take tea with your long-dead grandmother, lucky you. But that might be a onetime thing. And in breath, "deeper" is by no means synonymous with "more psychedelic." It's possible the most profound effect of a breathwork

6

Inhale

practice on the sober mind is its power to provide a safe space to work through long-held resentments, release past trauma, and access the energy required to live life clean and clear, and hopefully, with a lot of joy.

6

Drugs

7

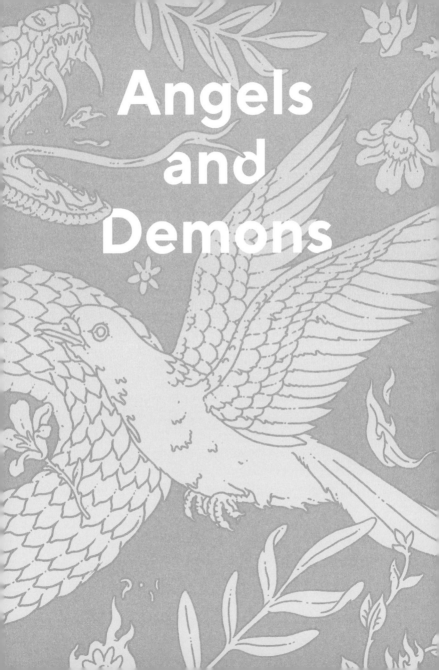

Angels and Demons

When you lie down and let go—

really let go—

you should expect visitors.

These messengers can come in many forms—
from abstract premonitions to crystal-clear
realizations to figures from your past to
otherworldly beings.

For our purposes, we're defining angels and
demons in the broadest terms possible, as
guardians or messengers and sources of
distress, respectively.

Some receptive breathers will get the
heavenly light, wings, robes, and harps
experience and a radiant visit from Uriel,
Raphael, or Gabriel—but most won't.

Inhale

WHILE BREATHING, YOU MIGHT SENSE AN

otherworldly presence

OR AN ATTUNEMENT WITH AN

elevated energy

THAT POINTS YOU TOWARD

greater understanding of love

and life.

You may receive dreamlike visions of childhood pets, or wolves, or Sioux braves, or nineteenth-century Bavarian ancestors. These are just a few examples of the kind of myriad guardians your unique subconscious might serve up.

In this altered state, your guardians may deliver very clear messages or they might be signals slathered in symbolism. A leaf isn't always just a leaf when your long-gone grandmother hands it to you. It might be an

7

Angels and Demons

invitation to grow. Whatever comes up, pay attention, listen. You can cultivate your willingness to receive by breathing more deeply into the blocks that impede the channels between what is distinctly you and the subconscious, between self and realms ethereal. Communing with your better angels can be an illuminating, euphoric experience.

But being open to the light also leaves us open to the darkness. And there's light and darkness in all of us. There's a chance—after breathing for a few minutes— you might be confronted by your demons. This may present itself in the form of resistance: resistance to letting go, resistance to going deeper, resistance to feeling, resistance to understanding.

A demon may come in the simple form of the horror of reality. You may suddenly see yourself for exactly how you really are. Or you may become acutely aware of your role in a painful relationship that can no longer be blamed on the other person alone. In the breath, your BS will find you. In this sense, breathwork can be a lot like talk therapy, which reveals your operating system to you. It may become immediately apparent that, "Oh, shit, I'm a control freak" or "Oh, wow, I can't let myself just be for even one second" or "Oh, nuts, I'm addicted to sex, drugs, alcohol, ice cream, Instagram, etc." or "Oh, man, I'm attached to my role as the victim."

The ego likes to keep things intact, "as is," status quo. The ego's job is to keep the machine moving forward, not to explore the depths of consciousness. You may confront a powerful force hell-bent on keeping you stuck. For some reason, stuck feels safer. Your ego is an expert at constructing protection mechanisms. In its unrelenting pursuit of self-preservation, the ego builds fortresses of energetic scar tissue around old wounds.

IN BREATH WE CAN EXPOSE THOSE WOUNDS. You may be thinking, "Why would I want to do that?" Because in revealing our past traumas, we give them a chance to heal.

For others, demons come in the form of dark matter, entities that have entrenched themselves somewhere in the body, usually with a purpose. Perhaps it's something you were born with, handed down in the ancestral DNA. Or maybe it's something you picked up along the way. Whether sourced from your epigenetics or elsewhere, these demons can be cunning.

When this stuff—and stuff like it—comes up, be gentle with yourself. Awareness is half the battle.

7

Angels and Demons

The next step is definitely not to take down the psychospiritual samurai sword hanging from the wall and slaughter your demon. You'll lose. And, in the throes of battle, you'll probably end up slaughtering some of the soft, squishy self.

Instead, get to know your demons. Ask them why they're here, when they got here, and what they're doing for you. It's very possible that at some point in your life you needed this entity to survive. Thank them for that. Maybe even give them a compliment. Then make a plan with your demon to take back some of the power, share some of the load, let another aspect of you take the wheel. A trained facilitator can help you create a dialogue with an entity, to guide you to making it right-sized, put it in its right place, or release it when its job with you is complete.

This is life's-work kind of stuff. Not exorcism. So be patient, be compassionate with yourself, and keep breathing!

BREATHWORK ISN'T

all rainbows and unicorns.

IT CAN BRING

intense emotional discomfort.

Healing hurts. But it's worth it.

7

Angels and Demons

Exhale

Holotropic
Breathwork

Who needs it

Ayahuasca devotees, Burners, sober folks looking for a "freelapse," Pisces and Aquarians, anyone looking for a major breakthrough.

When to do it

When you are ready to scour the depths of your subconscious. When you have thirteen hours and hundreds of dollars to dedicate to an entire day of self-examination, depth psychology, and healing.

What it is

Holotropic Breathwork is a trademarked modality developed in the 1960s by pioneering psychiatrist and LSD researcher Stanislav Grof.

7

SIMPLY PUT,

Stanislav Grof believed that if achieving an altered sensory experience was possible with drugs, it must also be possible without them.

The brain receptors are there. They just need to be activated. And, after LSD was widely banned in the United States in the late 1960s, he developed Holotropic Breathwork to prove it. In fact, Holotropic breath is so connected to the psychedelic movement, that it's perhaps *the* breathwork modality for these consciousness-bending times.

Like LSD, Holotropic Breathwork is not for the faint of heart. It can be dramatic and unbalancing, and induce a total upheaval of self. It's comprised of deep inhales, followed by deep exhales, taking care not to allow any gap or break between inhale and exhale, exhale and inhale. It's hard to believe that just breathing with intensity—with inhales that fluidly become exhales and vice versa—can induce the kinds of experiences it does; but show up in Topanga Canyon for a Holotropic Breathwork workshop offered there, and any doubts will be quickly—and often resoundingly—dismissed.

This kind of breath with no end, no clear distinct break between inhale and exhale, is extremely powerful. I've heard Holotropic Breathwork described as the Super Bowl of breathwork. A typical Holotropic session is an all-day thing. It includes three hours—yes, three hours—of intense breathing, loud music curated to move you along on your psychedelic journey, followed by mandala drawing, and then a sharing circle intended to reground you and prepare you for reentry into civilization.

After arrival, you will find a partner, who will stay by your side the entire three hours you are breathing. Later in the day, you'll switch, "holding space" for your partner. If this sounds intense, it is. Most participants will begin lying on their back on a mat or pad, swaddled in a blanket, blindfolded with an eye mask. This womb-like setup provides comfort and total darkness to limit any external stimuli from getting in between you and your "trip." The facilitators take great care to make this a world without language, limiting any speech, verbal prompts, and recognizable lyrics in music to near zero. This is to ensure that your experience is not touched by external influence. As much as possible, Holotropic Breathwork is designed to be a journey into self, and self alone.

So, what might you find there while delving into the depths of your subconscious?

You may experience illusions or dreamlike narratives in which you—or some idealized version of you—are cast as the hero of your own legendary saga. You may be an active participant in interactions with archetypal figures, gatekeepers, otherworldly beings, or animal spirits. You may also find yourself in the role of the watcher, observing scenarios from a distance that seem written into your ancestral coding. Similar to the effects of smoking the intense "dream drug," DMT, you may witness radiant abstractions of prismatic color and light.

You may hear guttural growls or primal screams from other breathers around you. And you may feel emotions coming up and want to express them, too. You are encouraged to let it all out. If tightness or pain comes up, your partner may call over one of the trained bodyworkers on site, who will apply pressure to the affected area while you push, squirm, and scream it out.

YOU MIGHT EXPERIENCE
A TRANSCENDENT BODY HIGH.

As you lose track of time and the world around you, you may experience something akin to an out-of-body experience, where you are inseparable from the sensation itself.

YOU BECOME
pure unfettered ecstasy.

After breathing, you'll have an opportunity to draw, eat something, and share your experience. After listening to the stories of other breathers, you'll realize each person's experience is different. When it's all over, you might feel extremely raw, fragile, vulnerable, and open. When you commit to Holotropic breath, you are committing to going deep into the abyss. Make no mistake, this is depth psychology. It's about healing your deepest wounds, revealing your most painful traumas. If you suffer from any psychiatric conditions, you should definitely talk to your doctor before trying Holotropic Breathwork. It is very important to be extremely gentle with yourself in the days following a Holotropic Breathwork "sit," as the practitioners describe a session where you take turns sitting with a partner. Due to the intensity of the Holotropic experience, you may not be in a hurry to lie down and do it again anytime soon. Give it time to settle. You will have more perspective as the experience integrates into your psyche and you integrate yourself back into polite company.

In the months following an intense Holotropic Breathwork experience, you may find that you are less prone to negative thinking and better equipped to deal with the people, places, and things that have historically been triggers for resentment, stress, and anxiety. It can feel as if you took out your core issues, had a good look at them, realized you don't really need them, and just left them behind in the room. And that can be well worth the price of admission, usually a couple hundred bucks.

Unlike other modalities described in this book, you can't just lie down and "do" Holotropic Breathwork on your own. (Holotropic Breathwork is *only* Holotropic Breathwork under the guidance of a certified facilitator trained in Grof's method.) But you can head to Los Angeles for a full-day breathing experience, or find the community offering Holotropic experiences nearest you. Michael Stone, founder of Holotropic Breathwork Los Angeles, also offers online guidance through Neurodynamic Breathwork, which you can find through the magic of Google.

FURTHER READING

Holotropic Breathwork: A New Approach to Self-Exploration and Therapy
by Stanislav Grof and Christina Grof

HOW TO

Holotropic Breathwork

Or something like it. Here are instructions for integrating Holotropic methods into your breathwork practice.

Step One

Make a playlist that features activating music without lyrics. Check out the work of musician and sound healer Jonathan Goldman for a general idea of the kind of frequencies and harmonics that can get you out of your head and into the breath. And play it loud.

Step Two

Use a blindfold. A light-canceling eye mask can encourage you to go deeper into breath.

Step Three

Lie down on your back and breathe vigorously through the mouth. Extend and deepen your inhales and exhales. Attempt to remove any gap or pause between inhales and exhales, exhales and inhales.

Step Four

Experiment with dropping into this breathing pattern whenever you're looking to go deeper or having difficulty getting into other breath modalities (for example, when practicing Wim Hof–style breathing or the three-part breath described in the following pages).

Step Five

Take time to ground yourself after breathing. Journaling or drawing can be an excellent way to integrate and diffuse what comes up in the breath back into your present, conscious state.

Step Six

Be gentle with yourself. Always.

Zen

Who needs it

The aesthetically inclined, the chronically overstimulated, Japanophiles, Virgos, overthinkers, extreme closet organizers, minimalists, vegans, those who appreciate the finer things in life.

When to do it

When the voice in your head gets loud. When it's time to simplify everything. When your priorities get out of balance.

What it is

Zen breathwork is like a Tom Ford suit. Simple, understated. But impeccable, timeless, containing multitudes. If you have one, you really don't need anything else.

BORN IN CHINA, REFINED IN JAPAN,

Zen is a school of Buddhism.

For most Westerners, Zen is a clumsily culturally appropriated state of mind also known as "chill." Or it's a vibe sourced from scanning the self-help bookshelves featuring countless titles like *Zen and the Art of Motorcycle Maintenance*, *Zen in the Art of Archery*, *Zen and the Art of Disc Golf*, *Zen and the Art of Public School Teaching* . . .

In fact, Zen is so *not* chill. It's a rigorous, difficult practice, taught—sometimes quite literally—at the end of a stick (a *kyosaku*, a wood slat applied with a quick strike between the shoulder blades to wake drowsy and dozing monks). Zen's renunciant way of life can take a lifetime to master.

Enter a traditional Zendo, a place for Zen meditation, and your first impression might be: Zen is so chic. The black robes. The hand-tailored *rakusu* hanging over the neck of Zen precepts, conveying commitment and care. The clean lines. The air of simplicity. The incense.

Candles and flowers on the shrine to Manjushri Bodhisattva, depicted astride a lion, spear and sword in hand. That these implements of war are at the threshold for "sitting quietly, doing nothing" shouldn't be lost on you.

In fact, should you choose the path of Zen, being armed against the demons in your own head—as opposed to defenseless and squirming—might prove extremely beneficial. Seated in silent meditation, just breathing, you may get graphic glimpses into the chaos of the mind.

Zazen is seated Zen meditation. It's the core of Zen practice and daily life. And it's all about the breath. Zen practitioners sit for thirty-five minutes and focus on the breath. Sometimes they count the breath. Sometimes they don't. They breathe through the nose with a gaze directed at nothing in particular. They place the tongue gently on the roof of the mouth. And they hold their hands in their lap in a cosmic mudra. They become very still. And then they get busy doing nothing.

It's said, "The practice is returning." So, if you're seated in Zen meditation and start making a shopping list, return to the breath. If you find yourself ruminating on how Becky slandered you at senior prom, return to the breath. If you catch yourself deeply fantasizing about Ryan Gosling, return to the breath.

EVEN ONE SESSION OF ZEN MEDITATION TEACHES US THAT WHATEVER IT IS, IT CAN WAIT.

It's about being totally present in the moment.

There are twenty-three hours and twenty-five minutes of the day to flail in the comings and goings of the mind's whims. But for the thirty-five minutes seated in zazen, that's it. It's just you and the *zafu* (meditation cushion).

As you sit, thoughts and feelings will try to get a hold of you. They'll text. They'll call. Some will try to kick in your front door. No need to judge them. They're just doing what they do. They want your attention more than anything. But, who told you you had to give it to them? You don't have to like your thoughts. But you don't have to dislike them either.

We won't even begin to try to get into the inner working of the holistic Zen experience. Way more qualified scholars and students have tried and failed. Zen philosophy is notorious for defying all attempts at description with mere language. To illustrate that fact, Zen practitioners work *koans*, riddles designed

Zen

6

to showcase the shortcomings of logic and break the mind of its dualistic thinking.

However, Zen is one of the few areas of this world where "beginner's mind" is exalted. If you feel intimidated walking into a new environment, that's normal. But there's magic in the not knowing, the not understanding. That rawness and naïveté is worthy of quiet celebration.

In the beginning, try to focus on the experience of just being, just sitting.

If you're feeling that the Zen way is the way for you, ease into it before going full Leonard Cohen, joining a Zendo, slipping into a robe, taking the bodhisattva vows, and donating all your worldly possessions to Goodwill. Read some D. T. Suzuki. Read some Alan Watts. Find a Zen center in your hometown. Take an introductory Zen class. Go on a Zen meditation retreat. Enjoy being a beginner. If you can take one thing away, it's that in our daily efforts to be experts at everything, we lock ourselves out of any real opportunity to be a master of anything.

MASTERY TAKES TIME.
Real understanding takes time.

If you can get comfortable with the existential horror of not knowing, you may be able to get comfortable with anything—maybe even enlightenment.

Zen

6

FURTHER READING

The Way of Zen by Alan Watts

HOW TO
Zen

Step One

Find a nice comfortable cross-legged seat, perhaps on a zafu; or kneel on a *zabuton* (a small wooden bench that allows you to some-what comfortably perch atop your knees and shins). Set a meditation timer.

Step Two

Place your hands in the cosmic mudra. To do this, place the left hand inside your right hand, both palms facing up. Then, ever so gently touch the tips of thumbs together. Hold this mudra just below the navel.

Step Three

With the mouth closed and the tip of the tongue gently pressed to the roof of the mouth, begin to breathe in and out through the nose. There's no need to control or alter the breath in any way.

Step Four

Continue to breathe, eyes open, softly gazing forward and down. Do your best to remain completely still—and awake!

Step Five

When the mind wanders, return to the breath.

Step Six

When the mind wanders, return to the breath.

Step Seven

Repeat steps five and six until you're saved by the bell.

Pranayama

Who needs it

Seekers of enlightenment in the everyday
and mundane, the overworked and
overstressed, anyone looking to take their
yoga practice to a higher level.

When to do it

When you're feeling frazzled or anxious,
when it's time to get grounded before
embarking on a spiritual quest, when
you're looking to maximize the mind–body
connection of yoga's moving meditation.

What it is

If you've ever taken a yoga class, you've
likely done some kind of pranayama. The
traditional *ujjayi pranayama* (also known
as "victorious breath" and "ocean breath") is
fundamental in the practice of Ashtanga and
Vinyasa yoga.

Pranayama **is Sanskrit**

for "breathwork" or, literally,

"life force" (*prana*) "control" (*yama*).

For our purposes here, we're talking about any of a number of specific ancient breathing techniques that have come out of the yogic tradition, some of which have found their way into Buddhist meditation practices and even into Navy SEAL training.

With such a wide variety of options, pranayama is a bit like a new-age pharmacy of breath, with something to remedy whatever ails your spirit. If you're feeling overheated, angry, or too passionate, there's a pranayama technique for that. If you're feeling off-kilter and unbalanced, there's another pranayama technique for that.

And while pranayama can be intense, it can be a lot less intense than some of the other schools of breath described in these pages. This makes pranayama excellent for daily maintenance—not going too deep while still shaking off some nervous energy and getting present and calm for whatever lies ahead. It's easy to experiment. Try preparing for a big meeting or presentation at work with five minutes of "box breathing" (outlined on the next page). Then try it without. See what gets better results.

Pranayama techniques can give much-needed structure to your meditation practice. Those who struggle with the idea of "just sitting" can benefit from having something to do (i.e., adhering to a distinct pattern of breath). This can help you get out of "monkey mind" and into a kind of focused trance.

You can also drop into some quieter pranayama techniques stealth-style, implementing box breathing, for example, in a stressful situation without letting anyone around you even know you're doing it. Having subtle breathing techniques at your employ at all times can vastly improve your sense of well-being. No matter where you are or what you're doing, you'll always have access to your "chill zone."

Following, I outline the ins and outs of three pranayama techniques—box breathing, alternate-nostril breathing, and lion's breath.

FURTHER READING

Light on Prānāyāma: The Yogic Art of Breathing by B. K. S. Iyengar

Box Breathing

(Samavritti)

Implement box breathing whenever you need to reduce stress, improve focus, get grounded, and find a sense of calm in nerve-racking situations.

Step One

Find a nice comfortable seat. Sit up straight. Close your eyes. Relax your shoulders.

Step Two

Inhale through the nose as you silently count: *one, two, three, four.*

Step Three

Hold your breath at the top (full lungs) as you silently count: *one, two, three, four.*

Pranayama

5

Step Four

Exhale though the nose as you
silently count: *one, two, three, four.*

Step Five

Hold your breath at the bottom (empty
lungs) as you silently count: *one, two,
three, four.*

Step Six

Repeat steps two through six until
you feel grounded, with a sense of
balance, equanimity, and calm.

Step Seven

Practice. Experiment with longer counts
and holds, taking care to make sure each
side of the box is of equal length (inhale,
hold, exhale, hold).

Alternate-Nostril Breathing
(Nadi Shodhana)

Try alternate-nostril breathing whenever you want to balance the brain, improve your circulation, and calm a racing mind.

Step One

Take a comfortable seat, spine straight. Place your left hand in your lap.

Step Two

With your right hand in front of your face, place it in the traditional Vulcan salute (your index and middle finger should be squeezed together and—separately—your ring and pinkie fingers should be stuck together). Bring the tips of your index and middle finger to rest at the base of your thumb. Keep your

Pranayama

5

ring and pinkie fingers extended.
This is called *mrigi mudra*.

Step Three

Close off your right nostril with your thumb
and slowly inhale through your left nostril.

Step Four

Close off your left nostril with your ring
finger and pause.

Step Five

Remove your thumb from your right nostril
and slowly exhale through your right nostril.
Pause.

Step Six

Inhale slowly through your right nostril.

Step Seven

Close off your right nostril with your thumb
and pause.

Step Eight

Remove your ring finger from your left nostril
and slowly exhale through your left nostril.
Pause.

Step Nine

Inhale slowly through your left nostril.

Step Ten

Repeat steps four through nine.

Lion's Breath

(Simhasana Pranayama)

Use lion's breath to literally blow off some steam,
let go of anger and fiery thoughts, and relieve
tension in the jaw and the neck.

Step One

Sit atop the knees and shins or in a
cross-legged "easy pose."

Step Two

Inhale deeply through the nose.

Step Three

Open the mouth wide, push your tongue out
and down, gaze up, press the palms into your
knees, and push out the breath with an audible,
guttural exhale.

Step Four

Repeat steps two and three until
you feel cool, calm, and collected.

Step Five

Don't take yourself so seriously.
Let yourself roar.

Three-Part Breath

Who needs it

Artists, writers, lovers, naturalists, the grieving, those desperately needing to grieve, healers, the healing, people with mommy/daddy issues, anyone with resentments to shed.

When to do it

When the heart feels tight or closed. When the self-imposed boundaries to success become insurmountable. When you have thirty minutes to create a safe space, burn some sage, lie down, and make space for spirit.

What it is

The three-part breath is a pranayama technique. In theory, it's super simple. Lie down on your back, open your mouth, and breathe in three distinct actions:

1. Breathe into the belly.
2. Breathe into the chest.
3. Exhale.

And, repeat. This "stacking" of the breath gets energy moving. And fast.

WHILE EVERYONE WILL HAVE AN EXPERIENCE UNIQUE TO THEM, after just a few minutes of this breath pattern, the body will often begin to feel very different— often tingly.

As the blood becomes more oxygenated, energy starts moving, and the heart begins to open.

In this more receptive state, you can expect messages from realms ethereal, visitors from the subconscious, an outpouring of emotion (in laughter and tears), a feeling of pure unconditional love, and sometimes total elation.

In the first few minutes of breathing, you may also find this "simple" work extremely difficult. You may be resistant to letting go of control, going deeper into your somatic nervous system, and feeling sensations long buried. Real fears can bubble up. Fears of disappearing, fears of being exposed.

THE VOICE THAT MANAGES YOUR MIND MIGHT SAY, "I DON'T WANT TO."
This is totally normal.

The work here is pushing through this resistance, breaking the chains that bind you to the only experience of life you already know. And, if you can overcome your fears here, you can overcome your fears anywhere. If you can reveal the roots of your struggles, you can grow.

With practice, you might become aware of awakening energy centers starting to spin in your body. And you might also find those aforementioned lobster claws, rendering your hands temporarily useless. Tightness in the body during the three-part breath is normal. Tightness in the jaw? That might be a story you aren't telling or a song you aren't singing. That stiffness in your neck? That could be a romance you're hung up on. Pain in the right leg? That might be dissonance in the relationship with your father.

Do keep in mind: Not all energies are completely "yours" in the traditional sense. Some energies are picked up along the way. Some seem written in your ancestral coding. The three-part breath is about reclaiming what's yours and removing what's not.

If someone is "holding space" for you (i.e., quietly observing your body while you breathe), they'll see where energy is blocked and might encourage you to send your attention there with a vocal cue or applying pressure to the area with the touch of a hand. Often, people are blocked in the throat—where a lifetime of "holding in" feelings, keeping quiet, and not speaking their truth can get trapped—and in the lower pelvis, where creativity unexpressed or sexual trauma (or shame) can get stuck. Breathing into these areas can be immediately liberating or can take time—many sessions—to work through.

The release from breaking through these blocks can result in enlivened feelings of exaltation—a kind of psychedelic upheaval—or even send you into a deep, dreamy kind of sleep known as *yoga nidra*. There seems to be no quicker, more efficient, less expensive, less toxic way to achieve an altered state than the three-part breath.

The fact that the three-part breath is practiced and taught in new-age communities from coast to coast and around the globe seems in large part due to the work of Los Angeles–based healer David Elliott. Elliott has taught the three-part breath to hundreds of healers around the city, nation, and world.

Elliott's philosophy is a holistic one, grounded in taking responsibility for your own experience, developing your intuition to heal yourself and others, and drawing—where appropriate—from Eastern and Native American spirituality. Elliott integrates sage, sweet grass, essential oils, and minerals from the earth into his healing sessions, as do his acolytes. This is something you might choose to do to add a bit of sacred ritual to your breathing experience.

Before engaging in healing work, Elliott suggests you ask yourself, "Am I clear?" Is my heart open?" The theory is that any interaction, relationship, project, or creative endeavor would benefit from you coming at it open to possibility with a defogged mind-set.

IT'S HARD TO IMAGINE ANY SITUATION WHERE YOU WOULD WANT LESS CLARITY, LESS COMPASSION.

So that's the drill here—

preparing yourself for your

life's love and work, one

breathing session at a time.

4

FURTHER READING

Healing by David Elliott

HOW TO
Three-Part Breath

Step One

Claim your space. Set the mood. This can be achieved by laying a mat on the floor, burning sage, lighting a candle, playing music, drumming, etc. An eye mask or weighted eye pillow is a nice to have, as is a blanket, as the body may experience fluctuations in temperature as you begin the breathing.

Step Two

Ground yourself. This can be achieved by making a concerted effort to feel all of your body parts, feet to skull; anointing the body's energy centers with essential oils; making a gratitude list; holding on to some grounding minerals like hematite, garnet, or smoky quartz; or just making conscious physical contact with the ground beneath you (i.e., literally touch the ground, tune in to it, feel it).

Step Three

Lie down flat on your back. It's best not to prop up the head on a pillow, as a bend in the neck can close off the throat, creating an impasse between heart and head.

Step Four

Open your mouth, all the way. Relax your jaw to open it wider.

Step Five

Breathe into your belly. Breathe into your chest. Breathe out. Breathe into your belly. Into your chest. Exhale. Belly. Chest. Exhale. This might help you to take in more air: Imagine your belly at diaphragm level and your chest where your collarbones meet your shoulders.

Step Six

Repeat step five for a preset amount of time; twenty minutes is a good place to start. If you lose your rhythm or find yourself not breathing, remember: Belly. Chest. Exhale.

NOTE: Some people breathe athletically, chest heaving, like a locomotive. Others, more slowly. There isn't a right or a wrong way to breathe. Fast and hard or slow and steady—whatever fills you up, go with the flow.

Step Seven

At the end of vigorous breathing (the active, *yang*, masculine approach to breath), return to a normal, quiet breath through the nose (i.e., the more receptive, yin, feminine approach to breath). Do this until you feel grounded again; maybe ten minutes.

Step Eight

Reground yourself. Stretch.
Drink some water.

Step Nine

Be alert. In the hours and days that follow a
session, you may notice little synchronicities
or encounters with the animal world—perhaps
in the form of hawks or hummingbirds flying
closer than usual. Make a note of them.
Mother Nature may have your back more
than you give her credit for.

The
Wim Hof
Method

Who needs it

CrossFit buffs, paleo and keto dieters,
extreme athletes, mountain men,
mountain women, lifehackers, survivalists,
neuroscientists, any Aries, the data driven.

When to do it

When it's time to muscle out the mayhem
in your mind. When you've just gotta get
those primordial juices flowing. When
you're in a hurry.

What it is

If ever there was a living legend of breathwork,
that legend is Wim Hof. The Dutchman
better known as the Iceman holds twenty-
six Guinness World Records and boasts
superhuman accomplishments of body and
mind that he guarantees you, too, can do.

3

"Feeling is understanding"

makes him the perfect antihero

for this mind-over-matter era.

Infectiously charismatic, Wim Hof is like a cross between a Spartan warrior from the movie *300* and the maniacally energized late comedian Robin Williams. He's climbed Everest in shorts. He's run a marathon in the Namib Desert without water. And he's submerged himself in ice for a record one hour, fifty-two minutes, and forty-two seconds. He counts super surfer Laird Hamilton and super producer Rick Rubin among his community. You may recognize Hof from zeitgeist appearances on Vice television and the *Joe Rogan Experience* podcast. And he's on a mission to bring "strength, happiness, and health" to the whole motherfucking world!

It can be difficult to watch Wim Hof in action without wanting to be Wim Hof. To accomplish that feat, one would have to wholeheartedly adopt the three pillars of Hof's signature method: cold therapy, breathing, and commitment.

BREATHWORK IS ALWAYS A SIMPLE TASK, BUT NEVER AN EASY ONE.

So, for many, Hof's force of will is both totally inspiring and totally worth modeling.

Without commitment and a drive more powerful than the resistance (resistance that will always say, "Breathwork? No, buddy. Not today.") we won't get up the *oomph* to actually do the breathwork. As for working ice baths and nearly nude alpine excursions into your daily practice, let's leave it to the icing Dutchman who says, "a cold shower a day keeps the doctor away."

Wim Hof breath has a lot in common with the Tibetan Buddhist tantric practice *tummo* (literally, "inner fire"), designed to generate inner heat while honoring the divine feminine. Every inhale is full, powerful, with intent. Exhales are an act of surrender, letting go. This interplay of big, bold inhales overpowering exhales has the result of leaving a surplus of oxygen in your blood. And it's that surplus that feeds your red blood cells and gets you feeling at one with the primal beast within.

Where Wim Hof breathing diverges from many modalities is in both the presence of long holds (or retentions) and the efficiency of the task at hand. You can get where you need to go (i.e., to oxygenate and alkalize the blood) in just fifteen minutes.

Holding the breath can be euphoric. It can be a display of endurance. And it can be an anxiety-inducing experience. However, if you can teach your body to relax around that sensation of needing something immediately, even painfully, you may be able to teach your body to do anything. That's the promise of the Wim Hof method. It's not too difficult to see how that can easily translate to other areas of your life (e.g., getting comfortable with delayed gratification, staying calm in stressful situations, and sticking with discomfort long enough to get to the great rewards life might have in store for you on the other side). It's here (and in the ice bath) that we begin to neutralize stress, and to fight back against what Hof calls "the terrorist in your mind."

From an efficiency and efficacy standpoint, Wim Hof breath is ideal for today's to-do-list lifestyle. It's easy to integrate into a daily routine (along with those cold showers). Thirty inhales and exhales. Then one big inhale and hold. Three times. That's a total of just ninety-three breaths. Taking ninety-three breaths before heading to the office in the morning isn't that daunting of a proposition, is it?

And, for all the data hounds, your progress is trackable. As you get happier, healthier, and stronger, you'll be able to hold your breath longer. The stopwatch becomes your friend. You may be astounded how long you can hold your breath in your first session of Wim Hof breathing. But, stick with it for a few weeks or months, and you may have some stats with which to really shock and awe your rock-climbing buddies.

If you want to dive deeper into the Wim Hof method— it's the twenty-first century, of course—there's an app for that. You can also take courses online, or in person with Hof's acolytes and disciples around the world, or even learn from the Iceman himself at a stop on one of his world tours, at his home base in the Netherlands, or in snowy Poland—where you can join Hof for an icy climb to the summit of Mount Sněžka in nothing but your shorts.

FURTHER READING

Becoming the Iceman: Pushing Past Perceived Limits by Wim Hof and Justin Rosales

HOW TO

The Wim Hof Method

Step One

If you're sitting up, make sure you are in a safe space with no objects harder than a pillow around you. Even better, lie down. That way, should you feel lightheaded, you won't hit your head on an end table, a coffee table, a Tiffany lamp, a giant rose-quartz slab, or a subwoofer.

Step Two

Take a big inhale through your nose or mouth. Really fill up. Then let it go. Again, breathe all the way in. Then let it go. Focus on powering up with each inhale and "casually" exhaling. The idea here—physically and energetically— is to take in more air than you let out. You're trying to create a surplus of oxygen in the blood, so, really power up. Then, release. Do this thirty times.

Step Three

At the end of your thirtieth inhale, exhale completely. With your lungs completely empty, hold the breath out. Grab your stopwatch, and start timing. Relax your entire body and see how long you can go without breathing. There's no need to panic, the breath will be there for you when you need it. And, there's no need to be a hero. Success here is really in how much you can relax all the muscles in your body without holding any air in your lungs.

Step Four

When you absolutely must breathe, inhale deeply. Hold that breath at the top for ten to fifteen seconds. Take a glance at the stop-watch and see how you did on that last hold. Then, exhale.

Step Five

Repeat steps two through four another two to four times.

Step Six

At the end of three to five total sequences, return to your normal breath pattern, kick back, and chill or meditate for a few minutes. Feel any sensations in the body. Soak up any feelings of warmth, love, and power emanating from within.

Step Seven OPTIONAL

Go run up a snow-capped peak in your underwear. *(At your own risk!)*

Kundalini

Who needs it

Scorpios, the chronically cleansing, spiritual seekers, anyone with creative blocks or sexual hang-ups they want to work through.

When to do it

When it's time to dissolve the ego, heal the soul, dare to get happy, create beauty, sleep better, chase rainbows, and find the joy in everyday life.

What it is

Kundalini is a school of yoga popularized in the West in the twentieth century with the arrival of Yogi Bhajan to the United States in the late 1960s. Kundalini yoga is a collection of ancient teachings, influenced heavily by Sikhism and Tantrism, and known as Raj yoga, or royal yoga.

WHILE IT MIGHT LOOK LIKE A RELIGION (OR A CULT, EVEN) TO SOME,

kundalini yogis often refer to their practice as a technology.

It's a "scientific system" designed to open the heart, stimulate the pituitary gland, and stretch the spine, awakening and cultivating kundalini energy. Kundalini energy is said to live at the base of the spine, coiled up in a dormant state like a snake. When awakened with breath, mantra, and movement, this energy will travel up the spine from tail to crown, unlocking our infinite creative potential. This buoyant energy—sourced neither from anxiety nor highly caffeinated cold brew—can be used to get things done.

Kundalini yoga is a system that some people will be inspired to dedicate their lives to—adopting an all-white wardrobe, covering the head, and committing to a vegetarian diet and a regimen of cold showers. For the rest of us, an every-so-often kundalini yoga practice can be integrated into a holistic approach to movement, breath, and health. Whereas an Ashtanga practice might be yoga to perfect the shape of the body, kundalini is yoga to perfect the shape of the soul.

BREATH—DETOXIFYING, LUNG-EXPANDING BREATH OF FIRE—IS ONE OF THE CORE TENETS OF THE PRACTICE. As Yogi Bhajan said, "The moment you are in touch with your breath, the universe pours into you."

A common refrain from devotees is: "Kundalini gets me high." This invigorating, intoxicating sensation is the result of vigorous movements and breath patterns that elevate the heart rate and create an inner heat. These movements are paired with the Sat Nam mantra, meaning "Truth is my name." Intense movement is followed by moments of rest, where the root lock (rectum, sex organs, and navel), or *mulbandh*, located at the perineum, is pulled up and in (think: Kegel exercises) and the breath is retained. It is here, in rest, that a euphoric sense of oneness with the universe finds us.

Each kundalini session is linked to a *kriya*, or "action," a series of sequential movements and meditations designed to elicit a different result. There are thousands of kriyas—kriyas for elevation, for conquering sleep, for balancing the organs, and for creating self-love.

Pairing mantra with breath, every kundalini class opens with the words, *Ong Namo Guru Dev Namo.* This translates as, "I bow to the creative wisdom, I bow to the divine teacher within." Kundalini yoga is about journeying inside the consciousness, observing what we find there, and discovering the infinite within the finite self. If that sounds a little too "woo-woo" for you, fair enough. But surrendering judgment and cynicism to the fire of breath might have you singing a different tune, namely, "May the Long Time Sun," a refrain sung by participants to close each class.

Kundalini yoga can be both physically and spiritually demanding. Its devotees claim rapid spiritual transformation. It can stimulate the libido. It can help prepare us for creative endeavors. With poses like "ego eradicator" and "fists of anger," kundalini yoga might be the ideal practice for our era of self-absorbed social media and political outrage.

Kundalini yoga is more than just stretching. It's a golden opportunity to get happy. Sat Nam.

FURTHER READING

Praana, Praanee, Praanayam: Exploring the Breath Technology of Kundalini Yoga as Taught by Yogi Bhajan by Yogi Bhajan

Kundalini

Before practicing any kundalini awakening movements and breath, it's a good idea to warm up the spine. You can do this (and avoid injuries) with a few minutes of alternating cat-and-cow stretches—getting onto all fours, flexing and curving the spine, broadening the chest cavity, and inhaling "Sat" and exhaling "Nam."

Fists of Anger

Use fists of anger to elevate your heart rate and release anger, anxiety, frustration, negativity, and stress from the system.

Step One

Sit up straight in a cross-legged pose.
Set a timer for three minutes.

Step Two

Place the tips of your thumbs at the base of your pinkies and ball both of your hands into fists.

Step Three

Inhale and exhale vigorously through an open mouth, pumping the navel with every exhale.

Step Four

Move the arms in a circular motion, drawing your fists in front of your face and over the back of your head. (Think: backstroke.)

Step Five

Visualize something you are angry about.

Step Six

At the end of three minutes, interlace the fingers above the head, press the palms up, stretch upward, and inhale.

Step Seven

Imagine white light all around your body.

Step Eight

Exhale.

Step Nine

Inhale.

Step Ten

Exhale.
Release the arms.
Relax.
Feel your feelings.

Ego Eradicator

Use ego eradicator to escape self-centered thought patterns, expand the lungs, and shake off cloudy confusion and mental fog.

Step One

Sit up straight in a cross-legged pose. Relax your shoulders. Elevate the arms above the head at a sixty-degree angle. Straighten the elbows. Curl the fingertips into the palms and extend both of the thumbs.

Step Two

Close the eyes and train your attention on the third eye (located in the center of your forehead).

Step Three

Begin breath of fire. Breath of fire is comprised of an even inhale and exhale through the nose, achieved by vigorously pumping the abdomen to force air in and out of the lungs. Focus only

on contracting and relaxing the navel.
Think of each inhale as a kind of involuntary
response to the power of the exhale. Find a
quick, staccato rhythm that challenges you.

Step Four

Continue with breath of fire for one to
three minutes.

Step Five

Inhale and bring the tips of the thumbs
together above the head. Hold your breath
at the top, pulling *mulbandh* (the root lock)
up and in.

Step Six

Release the fingers and lower the arms. Place
the hands in the lap. Rest.

Cooling Breath
(Sitali Pranayam)

Use *sitali pranayam* to cool and cleanse the body
and psyche, when feeling physically or emotionally
overheated.

Step One

Sit up straight in a cross-legged pose. Place
the palms on your legs. Curl your tongue like
a straw with the tip extended just outside
the lips.

Step Two

Inhale through your tongue.

Step Three

Exhale through your nose.

Step Four

Repeat steps three and four for three minutes.

Who needs it

A-types, goal setters, spiritual skeptics, control freaks, the attention depleted, the athletically inclined, anyone prone to anxiety and depression.

When to do it

When you have something to run away from; when you have something to run to; when it's time to get in shape; when you want to transform your body, mind, and the way you breathe.

What it is

Running is primal. The human body was made to run. Running isn't just for jocks and those prone to self-flagellation. The machinations and contorted postures of modern life have made it difficult for some to run without pain, but, with the right form and mind-set, running can be for everyone.

Running can also be a great source of spiritual strength.

It can be much more than point a to point b, much more than getting there faster than last time. It demands total presence in the moment. And, it demands breath. In this respect, running is a great metaphor for the spiritual life.

There's plenty of scholarship on cultures that have placed spiritual significance on long-distance running— from Bushmen in the Kalahari to the Navajo and Tarahumara tribes in North America to Buddhist monks in Japan and Tibet.

Sri Chinmoy, a renowned and widely followed Indian spiritual teacher who founded the Self-Transcendence 3100-Mile Race (described in the *New York Times* as "the Mount Everest of ultramarathons") said, "Run and become. Become and run. Run to succeed in the outer world. Become to succeed in the inner world."

Quite simply, running has the power to transform your life.

Studies show that even a small amount of running can combat depression.

And the health benefits of running are seemingly endless: Better sleep. More energy to take on the day's tasks. A leaner, more easily transportable body. Improved cardiovascular health. A faster, fat-burning metabolism.

RUNNING CAN ALSO DEVELOP THE BODY AS A VESSEL FOR SPIRITUAL DEVELOPMENT.

Running is spirituality, stripped down.

No gongs. No burning sage. Just you and the pavement ahead. If you commit to focusing on sensation and getting out of your head while you rack up the miles, you can arrive at some of the same enlightened destinations other breathwork practices listed in this book promise. In purest form, running connects you to the power of your breath.

Transforming your run into a breathwork session has three requirements: The first is diaphragmatic breathing. The second, exhaling on alternate foot strikes. And the third is meditation.

In running and in life, chest breathing is inherently limiting. It is way less efficient. And without contracting the diaphragm, there is less space for air, and you're siphoning off the amount of oxygen you can draw into the more efficient tissue of the lower lungs. When running, it's important to "belly breathe," or contract the diaphragm to broaden the abdominal cavity and power more air into your lungs.

To get a feel for diaphragmatic breathing, place your left hand on the belly and the right one on the chest. Take a deep breath. If the right hand moves first, try again. When you inhale, the diaphragm should move downward and your belly button should move outward. Concentrate on filling the belly with air instead of the chest until you get the hang of it.

Next, take your new and improved diaphragmatic breathing self out for a run. Here, you'll want to start exhaling on alternating foot strikes. This is extremely important for the preservation of the physical body and for faster post-run recovery. When the diaphragm relaxes on exhale, the core becomes less stable. When the core is less stable, the body bears more of the brunt force of foot impact. Landing on the same foot with every exhale effectively doubles the force of impact on that side of the body, making it more prone to the wear and tear of the road. Exhaling on alternate foot strikes essentially balances the force of impact across both sides of the body.

To exhale on alternating foot strikes, you'll want to breathe at a 3:2 ratio, counting 1-2-3 steps on inhales, and 1-2 steps on exhales. You can experiment with this lying on your back, tapping your feet. If you have a metronome handy, use it. Once you get into the rhythm, you'll find that every other exhale falls on a different foot. Take this breath pattern for a run.

Finally, bolster your spiritual strength by making your run a mindfulness practice. The diaphragmatic breathing and counting out the breath to alternate foot strikes will get you partway there. But make running a meditation, and you'll find you can run farther, faster, and with less pain. The key here is to clear the mind, let thoughts pass through you without attaching to them, and feel the sensations—both positive and negative—without assigning any judgment to either. As in any meditation practice, you'll get stronger and clearer with time.

Committing to a running routine—especially early in the morning—can add some monk-like discipline to your daily routine. If you need extra motivation, join a running club. There you'll find all the extra benefits of group energy's power to add accountability and motivation to any endeavor.

Regular cardiovascular exercise makes breathwork better. The lungs become more open and efficient, and you are more open to deeper experiences, on and off the pavement.

There are countless good reasons to run: To clear the mind. To find a balance of focus and relaxation. To release stress. To soak up the euphoric sensation of runner's high. But, mostly, run because it can be a great source of spiritual strength. If you can find your flow state in the high-impact, high-exertion environment of a run, you can likely find the flow state in anything.

FURTHER READING

Running with the Mind of Meditation:
Lessons for Training Body and Mind
by Sakyong Mipham

HOW TO

Running.
Yes, Running.

Step One

Set a goal, such as training for a half marathon or 10K. And remember to pace yourself, starting with short, slow runs and building upward.

Step Two

Wear the right shoes. Seriously. Find shoes that support the way you run.

Step Three

Before you run, meditate. Try box breathing (outlined on page 105) for ten minutes to quiet the mind and get focused before you lace up and go.

Step Four

Stretch.

Step Five

Run. Start slow. Breathe into the belly. And exhale on alternate foot strikes. To do this, you'll want to find that 3:2 ratio (i.e., inhaling for three steps, exhaling for two). With this ratio, your exhale will always fall on the opposite foot. As you pick up speed, you can experiment with a 2:1 ratio.

Step Six

Listen to your body. When it's time to rest, rest.

"When your breath is

shallow,

you are shallow.

When your breath is

deep,

you are deep."

—Yogi Bhajan

Acknowledgments

With special thanks
to David Elliott,
Ann Faison, Lauren
Spencer King,
Samantha Garrison,
Stacy Matulis, Tony
Giuliano, Eddie Ellner,
Carla Richmond
Coffing, Michael
Stone and Holotropic
Breathwork LA, Zen
Center of Los Angeles,
Wim Hof and Wim
Hof Experience,
Eric Nyquist, Rachel
Hiles, Lizzie Vaughan,
and the rest of the
Chronicle Books team,
and especially Eva
Sealove for breathing
beauty into every day.

Andrew Smart is a writer and creative director. He lives in Los Angeles, where he leads breathwork meditations. He is the author of *Crystals: The Stone Deck*.

Eric Nyquist is an illustrator based in Los Angeles, California.